RED GERARD

BY KAREN PRICE

SportsZone

An Imprint of Abdo Publishing
abdopublishing.com

abdopublishing.com

Published by Abdo Publishing, a division of ABDO, PO Box 398166, Minneapolis, Minnesota 55439. Copyright © 2019 by Abdo Consulting Group, Inc. International copyrights reserved in all countries. No part of this book may be reproduced in any form without written permission from the publisher. SportsZone™ is a trademark and logo of Abdo Publishing.

Printed in the United States of America, North Mankato, Minnesota
042018
012018

Cover Photo: Lee Jin-man/AP Images
Interior Photos: Erwin Scheriau/AFP/Getty Images, 4-5, 6-7; Han Myung-Gu/Getty Images Sport/Getty Images, 8-9; Sean M. Haffey/Getty Images Sport/Getty Images, 10-11; Shutterstock Images, 12-13, 16-17; Arina P. Habich/Shutterstock Images, 14-15; Hyoung Chang/The Denver Post/Getty Images, 18-19, 20-21; Clive Rose/Getty Images Sport/Getty Images, 22-23, 28-29; Martin Bureau/AFP/Getty Images, 24, 25; Tim Clayton/Corbis Sport/ Getty Images, 26; Mark Reis/Zuma Press/Newscom, 27

Editor: Patrick Donnelly
Series Designer: Jake Nordby

Library of Congress Control Number: 2018936261

Publisher's Cataloging-in-Publication Data

Names: Price, Karen, author.
Title: Red Gerard / by Karen Price.
Description: Minneapolis, Minnesota : Abdo Publishing, 2019. | Series: Olympic Stars Set 2
    | Includes online resources and index.
Identifiers: ISBN 9781532116063 (lib.bdg.) | ISBN 9781532157042 (ebook)
Subjects: LCSH: Olympic athletes--Juvenile literature. | Winter Olympics--Juvenile
    literature. | Snowboarders--Juvenile literature. | Medalists--Juvenile literature.
Classification: DDC 796.93092 [B]--dc23

CONTENTS

THE JOURNEY BEGINS

Red Gerard was just 16 years old. He had never won a big snowboarding competition in his life. But in February 2017, he was about to enter one of the biggest competitions of his career.

That winter day at Mammoth Mountain in California was the beginning of Olympic qualification season. Red needed to finish in the top three of the slopestyle event. That would give him a chance to go to PyeongChang, South Korea, and compete for Team USA in the 2018 Winter Olympics.

Red Gerard celebrates after finishing third at the Snowboard World Cup Slopestyle in January 2017.

Even though Red was young, he was already one of the best Americans in the sport. He'd also been getting better all season in slopestyle, his main event.

From a young age, Red could ride with snowboarders much older than him. He never had a problem keeping up. He has a reputation for riding with style and creativity. He also has great board control. He likes to stay loose and have fun. Red just loves to snowboard, and he always has.

Red is known for his laid-back, relaxed attitude on the course.

Going into the finals that day at Mammoth Mountain, Red was the top qualifier.

The people around him wished him good luck. Red focused his mind. Then he put his hands on his knees and took off down the mountain for his first run. He jumped up, flipped around, and landed on one of the rails. He hit a jump and flipped over backward. Soon he was cruising toward the big jumps.

Concentration and athletic ability both play important roles in snowboarding.

Red spun through the air three and a half turns and grabbed the tail of his board. On another jump, he spun two and a half turns the other way. He landed every jump. The judges rewarded him with a top score.

Red won the competition. He celebrated with his friends and family. But his work was not done. In fact, his journey to the Olympics was just beginning.

Red stands between Dylan Thomas, *left*, and Kyle Mack after taking first place in slopestyle at Mammoth Mountain.

FROM CLEVELAND TO COLORADO

Redmond Gerard was born on June 29, 2000, in a suburb of Cleveland, Ohio. "Red" was the youngest of five boys and the sixth of seven children. He started snowboarding when he was just 2 years old. His older brothers were snowboarders, and he tagged along with them. His brother Brendan said they all knew Red was going to be something special by the time he was 6 years old.

FAST FACT
Slopestyle snowboarders are judged on how hard their tricks are, how many tricks they do, and how well they land them. They are also judged on creativity and style.

Slopestyle was added to the Olympics in 2014.

Breckenridge Ski Resort provided Red and his brothers plenty of opportunities for practicing their skills.

Red's family moved to Colorado when he was 7. There weren't many mountains near his home in Ohio. His new home in the Rocky Mountains provided more opportunities to ride.

The Gerard brothers built a snowboard park behind their house. They used a tow rope hooked to the motor from a dirt bike. Sometimes they towed one another behind a four-wheeler.

Red liked to ride at the nearby Breckenridge Ski Resort. Then he would come home and ride some more. He and his friends learned new tricks and practiced on the rails and jumps they built.

Even though he was still young, Red was getting better every day.

Red began traveling all over the country for snowboarding competitions when he was 10 years old.

STAR ON THE RISE

Red began competing in snowboarding when he was 10 years old. He was 13 when he was named to the US Rookie Snowboard Team.

He kept improving his skills. A year later, Red advanced to the US Revolution Tour. That was just one step below the professional tour. He traveled as far away as Pennsylvania and California for competitions. He finished as high as second place, and he took fourth at the 2015 Junior World Championships.

By 2015 Red was ready to compete against the best. He made his pro slopestyle debut on the Dew Tour and placed fifth in his first competition. Then at the US Open, he finished in fifth place.

Though he was just 15 years old, Red had such a good year that he joined the US pro team. He was making a name for himself. But he still wasn't making it onto podiums at the top competitions.

Red relies on strength and balance to perform his tricks.

Red goofs around after clinching his spot on the Olympic team with a victory at the US Grand Prix in Snowmass, Colorado.

In January 2017, Red made his Winter X Games debut in Aspen, Colorado. He did not qualify for the finals. But he bounced back from that disappointment by winning his first big event in the competition at Mammoth Mountain.

After that Red knew the Olympics were within reach. On January 12, 2018, he needed to be the top American at the slopestyle competition in Snowmass, Colorado. If he could do that, he'd make the Olympic team.

Red won again. He was going to the Olympics!

RED SEES GOLD

Before Red could have a shot at an Olympic medal, he had to qualify for the final. That wasn't a given. The competition was tough.

Canadians Max Parrot and 2014 Olympic bronze medalist Mark McMorris were there. So was Norway's Marcus Kleveland, who had just won his second straight X Games competition. Norwegian Ståle Sandbech, the Olympic silver medalist in 2014, was back as well. They would all be hard to beat.

But Red wasn't nervous. He never is. Four Americans started, including Red. He was the only one who made it through to the final.

A drone keeps an eye on
Red during his qualifying
runs at the 2018 Olympics in
PyeongChang, South Korea.

Red spent the night before the final watching TV. The next morning, he overslept and couldn't find his jacket. He had to borrow one from teammate Kyle Mack.

The sky was clear, but a strong wind was blowing, making it tougher on smaller riders such as Red. On his first run, Red touched his hand down during a landing. The mistake gave him a low score.

Red's second run was not much better. He fell. The youngest snowboarder in the competition was in last place. He only had one chance left.

Red struggled during his first two runs of the final.

Red didn't hold anything back on his final run.

But Red stayed confident. After hugs and high fives with teammates at the top, Red started down the hill.

He glided through the rail section with style. His run was unique. Red approached the jump where he fell on the second run. He made three and a half spins while grabbing his board. He landed beautifully.

Red came to the final jump. He knew he could win a medal with just one more big trick and clean landing. His body corkscrewed through the air, around and around.

The landing was perfect.

With every twist and jump, Red moved closer to a gold medal.

When Red nailed the landing of his final jump, he knew he'd come up with his best run at the perfect time.

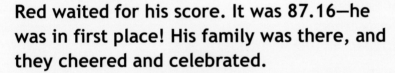

Red celebrates his victory in the slopestyle competition at the 2018 Winter Games.

Red waited for his score. It was 87.16—he was in first place! His family was there, and they cheered and celebrated.

More riders still had to go, but none would beat his score. Red had won the biggest snowboarding competition on the planet. The gold medal was his. It was the first medal of the 2018 Olympics for the United States. Red also became the youngest American snowboarder ever to win an Olympic medal.

Red's Olympics weren't over. He also finished fifth in big air. At just 17 years old, Red could be in line for many more medals in the future.

TIMELINE

2000
Red Gerard is born on June 29 in Westlake, Ohio.

2002
When Red is just 2 years old, he joins his older brothers and goes snowboarding for the first time.

2008
The Gerard family moves to the mountains of Colorado, where Red and his brothers build a snowboard park in their backyard.

2011
Red enters his first snowboarding competition.

2015
Red makes his professional snowboarding debut competing on the Dew Tour. He places fifth in his first competition.

2017
Red wins the Toyota US Grand Prix at Mammoth Mountain, California. It's the first qualifying competition for the 2018 Olympics.

2018
On January 12, Red wins another qualifying competition in Snowmass, Colorado, earning him a spot on the US Olympic Snowboarding Team.

2018
Red wins the gold medal in slopestyle in his Olympic debut on February 11. Thirteen days later, he places fifth in big air's Olympic debut.

GLOSSARY

competition
An event or contest at which snowboarders are judged and try for the highest score possible.

corkscrew
A trick in which a rider spins up and down in addition to side to side.

creativity
Using imagination to do something original and different from what others are doing.

Olympic qualifier
A competition that decides who will make the Olympic team.

podium
The box that athletes stand on to receive their medals or awards after placing in the top three at a competition.

rail
A long section of metal or plastic that snowboarders slide on.

slopestyle
An event in which snowboarders are judged for their tricks off rails, jumps, and other elements.

snowboard park
An outdoor area that features jumps, rails, boxes, and other elements that skiers and snowboarders use to perform tricks.

tow rope
A rope that skiers and snowboarders hold in order to be pulled back up a mountain.

unique
Different, one of a kind, not like the others.

INDEX

About the Author

Karen Price has lived in Philadelphia and Colorado and now calls Pittsburgh home. She has been writing about sports for more than 20 years.